Christopher Newport

by

Amy Williams Boykin

FOXHOUND PUBLISHING, LLC

Glen Allen, Virginia

1837 3603
A

The author wishes to thank Dr. Timothy E. Morgan of Christopher Newport University's History Department for his invaluable contributions to the preparation of this book.

Foxhound Publishing, LLC
P.O. Box 5543
Glen Allen, VA 23058
www.foxhoundpublishing.com

Produced by Shoreline Publishing Group LLC
Santa Barbara, California

Designed by Ox and Company, Inc.

Library of Congress
CIP Data Available

ISBN 1-58796-008-7

Printed in the United States of America

Contents

An Early Start

Captain Christopher Newport was an explorer, navigator, and adventurer. He sailed on many long ocean trips to the Caribbean, North America, and Asia.

Newport was born in 1561 and grew up in a part of London, England, known as Limehouse. Most of London's sailors came from Limehouse. It was not unusual for boys from 12 to 14 years old to work on ships. By the time he was a teenager, Christopher Newport was living and working on large sailing ships.

These drawings show the *Susan Constant*, one of the ships that Newport sailed to North America (see page 12). ▶

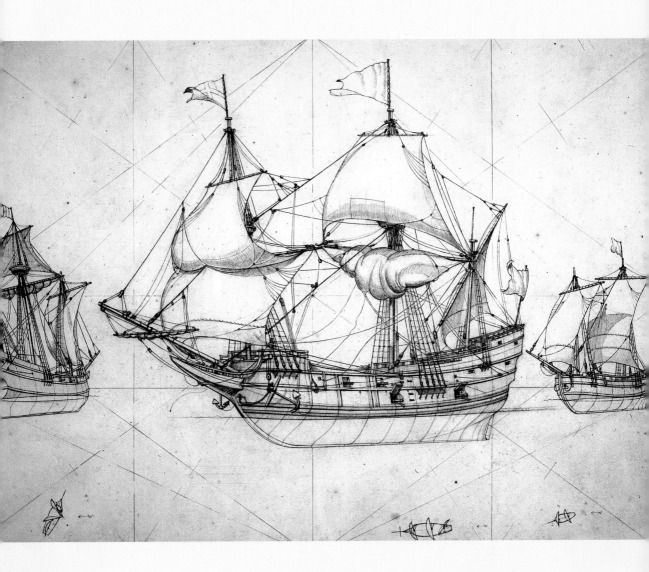

5

Off to Sea

In 1580, Christopher Newport left England and sailed as a **privateer**. A privateer is someone who has his government's permission to attack enemy ships and take their treasure. He sailed to the Caribbean, an area between North and South America. He also went to the South American nation of Brazil.

On a trip in 1590, Christopher Newport helped attack a Spanish treasure ship.

Newport was badly hurt during the battle off the coast of Cuba during a war between England and Spain. He lost his right forearm in the fight. Later, he used a metal hook in place of his right hand. He continued to sail and explore the oceans wearing his metal hook.

◀ This painting shows Spanish ships that sailed in Newport's time.

Peace on the Waters

Peace was made between England and Spain in 1604. Newport then made many more trips to the Caribbean. He traded with the Spanish on these trips and did not try to steal their silver and gold.

Newport returned from the Caribbean in September 1605. He went to London to meet with King James I of England. Newport showed the king a crocodile and a **boar**, a type of wild pig.

All these sailing trips helped Newport learn the sailing routes across the Atlantic Ocean to the New World. That was the name given to the place that today we call North America. Many European countries wanted to include parts of the New World in their **empires**, or lands they controlled.

This 1626 map shows what Europeans knew about the lands around the Atlantic Ocean. ▶

AMERICA
with those known parts in
that vnknowne worlde
both people and manner
of buildings Discribed
and inlarged &c. Ano 1626

THE UNKNOWNE WORLD

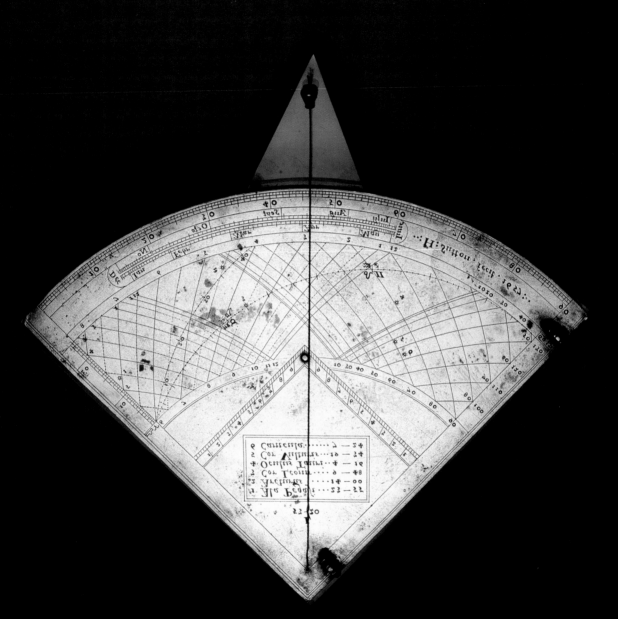

Finding Their Way Around

Sailors and navigators used many different tools to find their way, or navigate, on the ocean. The most important tools included the **compass**, the **astrolabe**, and a variety of staffs.

The compass was used to tell which direction the ship was going. On the ocean, the compass helped determine which way was east, west, north, or south.

The astrolabe was used to observe the position of the sun or points of light like the moon or the North Star. The staffs, or long poles, were used to measure the angle between the sun or North Star and the **horizon**. The horizon is the point where the water meets the sky. By taking these measurements, sailors could determine how far north or south of the equator they were. They could also decide which direction to sail.

◄ This is a quadrant, another tool sailors used to find their way.

Admiral Newport

Newport joined the Virginia Company, which was set up in 1606 by King James I of England. The Virginia Company's job was to bring settlers to the New World.

Christopher Newport was promoted to Admiral. He was put in "sole charge and command" of a journey to Virginia in 1606. This trip included 120

men and boys. They sailed on three English ships: the *Susan Constant*, the *Godspeed*, and the *Discovery*.

The explorers arrived in the Chesapeake Bay in April 1607. They built James Fort on the edge of the James River in what is now part of Virginia. James Fort was the first permanent English settlement in the New World.

This mural from Newport News (Virginia) Public Library shows Newport in the New World. ▼

Settling Jamestown

Christopher Newport left James Fort to return to England for supplies. He left some of the settlers in charge of the fort while he was gone.

The area around James Fort came to be called James Cittie. James Cittie later became known as Jamestown. Newport made three more trips from England to James Cittie between 1608 and 1611. He brought supplies and more than 440 people from England to live in that area.

Many people in England were looking for a new place to live. They wanted more room to spread out and more freedom. The New World was full of opportunities. The land was rich and would grow crops well.

◄ This scene shows the waterfront area in Jamestown in about 1619.

Meeting the Native People

In 1608, Christopher Newport was in Jamestown with John Smith, a leader of the settlers. Together, they visited with Powhatan, chief of about 30 local tribes of native people. Chief Powhatan's village was in a place called Werowocomoco. Newport and Smith returned to Jamestown from Chief Powhatan's village with a supply of corn to help feed the settlers.

There would be many more meetings between Native people and English settlers. In some cases, the groups worked together peacefully. English people learned much about their new land from the Natives.

This painting imagines John Smith ▶
meeting with Powhatan's people.

THE
TEMPEST,
OR THE
Enchanted Island.
A.
COMEDY.

As it is now Acted at His Highness the Duke of *York's*
THEATRE.

  Robert *Whilton*

LONDON,

Printed by *T. N.* for *Henry Herringman*, at the *Blew*
Anchor in the *Lower Walk* of the *New-Exchange.*
MDCLXXIV.

4

Shipwrecked!

There was a terrible storm in 1609, during Newport's third voyage to Jamestown. Newport's ship, the *Sea Venture*, was separated from the other ships on this trip. His ship was wrecked on Bermuda Island, but no one was hurt. Several months went by while the settlers built two new ships and continued their journey to Jamestown.

Soon, the story of Christopher Newport's shipwreck reached England. The famous writer William Shakespeare wrote a new play, called *The Tempest*, which may have been based on Newport's shipwreck story.

◄ This is the title page from a 1674 printed edition of Shakespeare's play *The Tempest*.

Newport left the Virginia Company in 1613 to join the East India Company. He began to sail and explore the lands and waters of Asia. Newport traveled from England to the East Indies, a group of island countries in the Indian Ocean. He carried people and cargo around the southern tip of Africa and on to a place called Bantam on Java. Java was an island that was part of the East Indies. It is now part of the nation of Indonesia. When Newport returned to England in 1614, he found that he had set a speed record for that type of voyage. He had sailed nearly 7,000 miles in about 500 days.

Tobacco was one of the most important crops that the New World sent to Europe. ▶

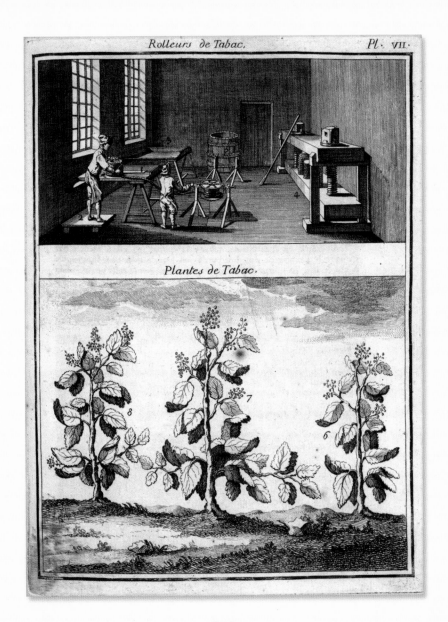

Rolleurs de Tabac.

Pl. VII.

Plantes de Tabac.

21

Newport's Last Voyage

Christopher Newport left England in 1616 as the captain of the *Hope*, a sailing ship. He arrived back in Bantam in August 1617, and died shortly thereafter. He had accomplished many things in his lifetime. He is best remembered for his journeys to the New World.

Without his sailing skills and leadership, English settlers might not have reached America or been able to settle there permanently.

This painting shows ships off the coast of Bantam on the island of Java.

Remember These Dates for Christopher Newport

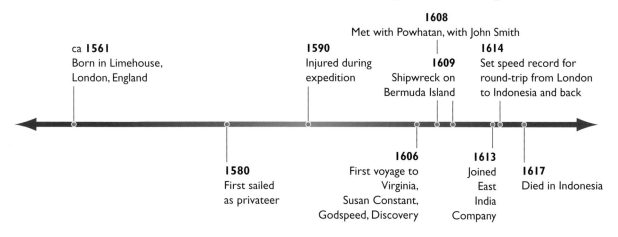

1608
Met with Powhatan, with John Smith

ca **1561**
Born in Limehouse,
London, England

1590
Injured during
expedition

1609
Shipwreck on
Bermuda Island

1614
Set speed record for
round-trip from London
to Indonesia and back

1580
First sailed
as privateer

1606
First voyage to
Virginia,
Susan Constant,
Godspeed, Discovery

1613
Joined
East
India
Company

1617
Died in Indonesia

Spend More Time with Christopher Newport

Web Sites

Captain Christopher Newport
*http://www.cnu.edu/library/
Newport.html*

Discoverers Web
*http://www.win.tue.nl/~engels/
discovery/*
Collection of links for information about
explorers, put up by Andre Engels, a
professor from the Netherlands

Books

Fritz, Jean, and Anthony Bacon Venti
(illustrator). *Around the World in
a Hundred Years: From Henry the
Navigator to Magellan*. Putnam
Publishing Group, 1994.

Johnstone, Michael. *The History News:
Explorers*. Candlewick Press, 1997.

Maestro, Betsy, and Guilo Maestro
(illustrator). *Exploration and Conquest:
The Americas After Columbus: 1500-
1620*. Mulberry Books, 1997.

Index

Photo Credits

Photographs:
Cover: Detail from the Christopher Newport mural painted by Allan Jones Jr. located in the West Avenue Library of the Newport News Public Library System, Newport News, Virginia (the full mural is shown on page 12); Mariners' Museum, Newport News, Virg.: 5, 6, 9, 10, 14, 21, 22; North Wind Archives: 17; Horace Howard Furness Memorial Library, University of Pennsylvania: 18.

About the Author

Amy Williams Boykin is a librarian and writer living in Virginia. She works at Christopher Newport University in Newport News, Virginia. She has written for library journals and has helped create Web sites about a wide variety of topics.